THE LOVE-SUICIDES
AT SONEZAKI

THE LOVE-SUICIDES AT SONEZAKI

AND OTHER POEMS

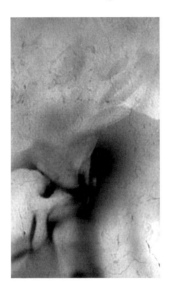

BY SIRI VON REIS

WITH A NOTE BY RICHARD HOWARD

Zoo Press

Grateful acknowledgement goes out to *The Paris Review*, where some of these poems first appeared:

"Glittering Ghost," "Luminist, National Gallery," "Quasi-Stellar Object," "The Very Large Telescope," "Vast Problem Still Obscure," "*The Love-Suicides at Sonezaki*," "Because They Live on Blood Alone, Vampires," "A Diet of Glass," "In Amber."

Zoo Press
P.O. Box 22990
Lincoln, Nebraska 68542

Printed in the United States of America

Produced and designed for Zoo Press by Compass Books
Minneapolis • Sioux Falls • Cover by Scott Stoel © 2001

Library of Congress Cataloging-in-Publication Data
    von Reis, Siri, 1931-
       The Love-Suicides at Sonezaki/ by Siri von Reis
         p. cm.
      ISBN: 0-9708177-2-X (alk. paper)
      1. Title.
      PS3622.O66 L6 2001
      811'.54--dc21

c 10 9 8 7 6 5 4 3 2 1

FIRST EDITION

for my teachers

Contents

III

IV

V

A Note on *The Love-Suicides at Sonezaki*

I find my accounting in our language: "deadpan" we say
when we invoke an expression of sarcasm, that stoical rever-
sal of intent, and indeed we use the nomenclature of mor-
tality, of lethality even, whenever our transactions are with
accuracy, with exactitude, and of course with the cool preci-
sions of irony: dead center, dead on, dead to rights, dead
ringer. It is the facts that Siri von Reis serves us, just the
facts, ma'am, and without discernable affect, the good
reporter allowing information to get through to us intact and
entire, deadpan indeed:

> Miss Mary Vincent says she still fears
> the man who raped her and cut off her arms.

This poet actually espouses the convention of the headline,
letting the title run on to become the opening of the "story"
to follow, not a word wasted, not a phrase for effect.
Deadpan indeed, yet there is nothing but life in the utter-
ance, the same telling simplicity as when Leontes says: "let
it be an art lawful as eating," or Caliban: "I must eat my
dinner."

I suspect that the poems have their ultimate effect because
we are shocked (thrilled?) by the violence done to the
expectations of prosody here, the abrupt substitution of
prose for a longed-for versification, especially at the close
of each elementary revelation:

> the sun about to disappear, the American
> sky vast and isolated, looking
> forward, looking back.

But that is merely—merely!—another way she has of estab-
lishing, of *enhancing* the conventions, thus to infract them,

thus to flout our expectations (after all, that is what a convention is, an anticipation fulfilled). A glance through these pages, a glimpse of the pervasive *façon* of these poems will suffice: the formality is hungered-for even as it is harrowed. And the violence is all internal, where the meanings are.

Siri von Reis has *at heart* (curious place for them to be) the interests of our most dedicated front page: science, crime, high art and pop culture. To them all she turns her deadpan attention, her quickened phraseology, and her reader is taken in—captured indeed—by such implacable formulations. We have been let in on any number of the world's secrets, and cannot but feel somewhat ashamed, somewhat exalted thereby.

—Richard Howard

I

Glittering Ghost

Hundreds came to pay tribute and to pick over more
than 22,000 objects: sequined vests, fur coats, goblets,
bedroom sets, vases, vitrines, dolls, limousines

and trucks. Willie Collins got candelabra and other
props for his Look-Alike Show. He tried on 30 outfits.
"Believe me, even the shoes are right."

Bob Nye, keyboard dealer from Reading, Pa.,
paid a fortune for the Baldwin with its gold-tufted
adjustable bench. "I've got the world's biggest

organ, and I resemble him." Mrs. Joyce Childers,
her hair in a beehive, came from Abilene. "If you'd ever
seen him in person, he made you feel as elegant

as *he* was." She remembers his stepping into
the audience to show his rings up close. "Do you like
these?" he would ask. "I'm so happy. You helped

pay for them." James 'Jimmy' Von Stodt of Long
Beach said only, "I loved that man". Mr. Von Stodt
was wearing an orange and white tank top, orange

cord shorts, white sandals, gold necklaces
and a diamond in his earlobe, under a hearing aide.
Mirror-faced, with a see-through lucite lid,

the Steinway, highlight of the sale, brought over
$42,000 by phone, from a London buyer. Another, signed
by the late owner, went to the National Museum

of Malaysia. Not allowed to bid, his brother's
widow hoped friends would be able to buy her the panda
Oriental rug that once adorned the Tivoli Gardens

Restaurant. "That's where we had our family dinners."
It took four days to knock everything down—with piano-
shaped paddles. Proceeds will be gathered to endow

A Foundation for the Creative and Performing Arts.

Available Soon in Stores, Judy,

the country's very first pregnant
doll, wears a denim maternity dress,

white tennis shoes and a wedding
ring. Even clever toddlers will be able

to help the ft.-high Mommy-to-Be
deliver an anatomically correct boy or

girl, with movable parts. Judy's
abdomen lifts off to pop the new baby

out, then flattens immediately.
(Little girls often stuff things into their

own underclothes or try to make
regular dolls look pregnant and pretend

smaller ones are their babies.)
Judy, though, has been called bizarre,

and a spokesperson for NOW now
says she conveys the distorted view

that women can look beautiful
and have babies all at the same time.

Tiny Tim, Who Collapsed while Singing

at a ukulele festival and died at 64 of heart
failure, was pear-shaped, beak-nosed,
long-haired, and Mannerist in dress.
He crooned '20's ballads in an age of acid,
strumming on a little instrument he'd pull
from a shopping bag.
Born Herbert Khaury
in New York City, he sang-along with radio,
idolized Rudy Vallee and fantasized about
a "once gay America full of music
and romance". A stand-out in white
Pan-Cake and tresses, he left George
Washington High
for talent contests,
discovered Jesus, prayed for a vocal style
and soon found the quavery falsetto
that became his trademark. "It was
easy on my throat, and I thrilled myself."
With his equally tremulous baritone, he also
created auto-duets.
As Larry Love, the Singing
Canary, he played the freak in Times
Square and worked gratis for clubs,
before getting paid at Café Bizarre.
Urged to change his name, he dropped
Julian Foxglove, Emmett Swink, a string of
other aliases and appeared at The Scene.
With a film
snippet, a record contract, and a stint on
'Laugh-In', he hit it big with a remake of
"Tip-toe Through the Tulips", then
"God Bless Tiny Tim", "Tiny Tim's
Second Album", and "For All My Little
Friends", which flopped.

During brief, heady
fame, his on-camera marriage to a teen-ager
captured an unprecedented TV audience
but didn't last. Touring with ever
fewer fans, he managed a spurt of
late releases, including "The Impotent
Troubador", "Tiny Rock",
and, recently,
a Xmas album. Critics, who first took him
for a fake, concluded he was an original,
a dreamer who believed
in the voices he said
lived in him.

The Sale Will Start with Little-

known Marilyn Monroe: for counter-
cards, to display Ansco Color Labs'

once new picture-processing,
young Norma Jean smiles from life,

demure in a school-girl shirt and
winsome white shorts on a glorious

day at the beach long ago. No
copies, no prints, no duplicates—

only the slides (Lots 1-9) survive.
On the same morning, a pair of Judy

Garland's ruby slippers will be sold,
one of a number from "The Wizard

of Oz". (Because of wear and tear
on shoots, clothing worn by the stars

was made in multiples.) Size 6B, kid-
lined, covered in rouge silk, hand-

sewn with thousands of crimson-
dyed sequins, each slipper has one

rhinestone-trimmed bow and 3 scar-
let bugle-beads. To muffle Miss

Garland's footsteps on the famed brick
road, they bonded her soles with felt.

A Composer Not Concerned with Melody,

harmony, rhythm or timbre, Alvin Lucier
creates environments from feedback.

He holds a bowl over a microphone, or tapes
a familiar song and plays it in a teapot

while varying the sounds by lifting the lid.
Lucier has written for magnets and

ostrich eggs and once persuaded brain-waves,
amplified by electrodes, to make tones

that activated accelerating tapes, causing
percussion instruments to vibrate.

In one performance piece, Lucier records
his description of a work, then plays

the recording while re-recording the reading
with its acoustical reflections, which

thus grow in ever more resonating sequence.
Though his extended, imperceptibly

transforming music can irritate listeners,
Lucier insists that, when he elevates

tiny effects into celebrations of inner
workings, sound and space entwine

and the physical world sings.

Though Morton Feldman Wrote Nothing

that was not beautiful, a few years after his death
he remains celebrated and unknown. Hugely
influential in some circles,

studied intently by younger composers, earning
'Feldmanesque' a place in the lexicon
of today's music, his work

—like *Piano Four-Hands*, *Vertical Thoughts II*,
as well as the gyrating, 4-hour *Second
Quartet* —is admired for

its distance from contemporary polemics
and for its quiet, lustrous harmony.
Casual listeners can

easily miss the developmental subtleties,
and the scale of the pieces makes
live presentations

a rarity. *Rothko Chapel*, an exception
despite the treacherous score,
stands apart from the rest

of Feldman's oeuvre: a half-hour sound
 -scape for viola, wordless chorus,
percussion and celeste, it is

among the loftiest, loneliest utterances
in 20th century music. The players
must be barely audible but

not feeble, while isolated chords and fragments
hover in a dense silence until, nearly at
the end, the violist releases a heart

 -breaking melody. Even in an imperfect
performance, like Saturday night's,
the effect is sublime.

At Ninety-Seven, the Inventor of the Theremin

is dead. Student of astronomy, physics, cello and music
theory, L. S. Termen (pronounced term-YEN) was

once chief of the section of electrical oscillators
at the Petrograd Physico-Technical Institute, where,

in 1920, he built the theremin, or etherophone. An early
electronic synthesizer, the instrument looked like a

radio-receiver box and was played by moving one's
hands in front of its two antennae. After demonstrating

the machine to Stalin, Einstein and Bruno Walter, Termen
came to the United States, gave 'etherwave' concerts,

won a patent, married Lavinia Williams of the First
American Negro Ballet, and, in his own new Theremin

Laboratories, created 1) the Terpsitone or 'theremin
ether-wave musical dance platform', on which body move-

ments evoke equivalent sounds, 2) the Rhythmicon,
commissioned by Chas. Ives for mixing several rhythms

simultaneously, and 3) a security system for Sing Sing.
Visiting the USSR in '38, Mr. Theremin, accused of

spreading anti-Soviet ideas, was sent to Siberia, where
he fell to devising high security, remote-control vehicle-

tracking programs and a mini-eavesdropping device
that secretly got him the Stalin Prize and, in 7 years,

a pardon, then a Professorship of Acoustics at the Moscow
Conservatory. When a notice in *The N. Y. Times* praised

his musicality, Termen was removed from the post
and spent his remaining days as a lab assistant.

Bela Bartok Will Be Going Home

forty-three years after he died here in
exile. The composer's sons, a retired r.r.

officer, and an engineer in Homosassa, Fla.,
agreed to sending their father nearer to

"those closest him in life". After a service
at the Community Church of New York,

the coffin will be exhumed and a plaque
left on the Hartsdale grave-site.

The remains will be shipped on the QE2,
then taken by motorcade through

France, W. Germany and Austria. Concerts
and recitals will mark the procession

in Cherbourg, Paris, Strasbourg, Munich,
Vienna. The cortège will be met

by the Hungarian Minister escorting it
to Budapest, where six streets now

bear Bartok's name. There, his coffin
will be laid alongside his wife's,

his mother's, and his aunt's. Bartok's first
wife is buried nearby, and his friend

Zoltan Kodaly lies in the same cemetery,
on the Buda side of the Danube.

Hungary's President and a Unitarian
bishop will officiate. As shifts in

office could occur, it's not certain
who'll deliver the eulogies.

Picasso Was Dubious When His Friend Virgil

Thomson asked him to sit for a musical
portrait. Couperin, Schumann and Elgar had
tried the genre, but Thomson's art was drawn
from life, like Gertrude Stein's free-

associative, one-sitting literary portraits.
Thomson, who had watched painters in Paris,
kept his subject five feet distant, sleeping,
reading or dozing—and silent, to foster

psychic transference. The results varied
greatly—from non sequitur inventions,
canons, fugues, pieces of proto-counter-
point and hymn tunes, to relentless

polytonal fantasies—a gallery of Copland,
Harrison, the Bowleses, H. Wiley Hitchcock
and John Houseman, along with Miss Peggy
Guggenheim, others and Picasso (a driving,

bitonal piano piece). Thomson only once let a
sitter speak: New York's Mayor La Guardia,
commissioned by André Kostelanetz & sketched
orchestrally at City Hall. Subjects frequently

were surprised. Gerald Busby, a downstairs
Chelsea Hotel neighbor, found himself hard
to play. Tony Tommasini, the composer's
biographer, posing in Thomson's apartment

on a steamy August day, had hoped for
something languorous, maybe Italianate,
but got a harsh, dissonant étude. These
can all be heard at the nine-hour concert,

'A Thomson Celebration', with 18 pianists.
The likenesses for violin will be thrown in,
with letters, reviews, films and panels
on dining with Thomson, a fabled cook.

Luminist, National Gallery

One could easily overlook his 60 placid paintings
in the current show. From 1840 until he
died, Fitz Hugh Lane focused

a topographer's eye on New England shorelines,
documenting calm in an era of big clippers,
swift yachts, steamships that jostled

three-masted merchant vessels in Boston's
crowded harbor. Steersmen and towns
in his early work—Gloucester

fishermen, the America's Cup race—
gave way to works stripped of
anecdote, all light, hush,

spirit: *Becalmed off Halfway Rock,*
The Western Shore with Norman's
Woe, Ipswich Bay, Christmas

Cove. In these, Lane painted what he saw
with care, showing banal events
in a bare-bone, spare

format reporting color—momentary,
diffuse, efflorescent. One sees
each boat begin to sail away,

the sun about to disappear, the American
sky vast and isolated, looking
forward, looking back.

II

Helium, Neon, Argon, Krypton, Xenon, Radon

are solitary. Rare, noble gases, stable and complete,
their energy levels, as well as their shells,

are filled. They have no electrons to share, to lend,
to part with, nor need acquire any. Only a

compound strongly prone to grab electrons can press
the solitary atoms of such a gas to donate its

own: Xenon can be united with platinum and fluorine
into a crystalline substance of no use,

though a triumph of synthesis. Three or so inert
elements can be forced to join with halogens—

but only in the presence of a powerful current.
The resultant compounds survive for

a fraction of a second, then break into
pulses of intense laser light.

Pioneer 12 Has Flashed Down, Deep and Inward,

toward the second planet from the Sun,
after gathering billions of data, historic samples

of the heavy atmosphere surrounding Venus.
Expected to orbit the heavenly body only for days,

in the end it circled for years, while portions
of the craft melted or were torn away

by the intense friction of passing into her
thick clouds at undreamed of speeds.

On its fateful errand, Pioneer glimpsed undulating
surfaces, sweeping valleys, breathtaking

plateaus, pristine craters and traces
of ancient ocean basins dating from the birth of

the planet. When, at last, the robot disappeared
behind her, its mission was officially

over, though remnants may survive, burning
slowly, till they are drawn or pulled

into the torrid Venusian skin.

Pluto's Motion Is Chaotic,

its orbit is unique—highly eccentric,
much inclined, and subject to variations—

characteristics compelling students of
the planet to pursue its evolution

through the Digital Orrery, a new computer
that integrates paths of the outermost

planets for an 800-million-year
period. The model shows that Pluto's chaos

is robust and unpredictable—a discovery
that makes it hard to imagine

the planet's origin, for its deviant
movement, pumping other bodies erratically,

signals chaos all around. The nature of
long-term motion remains undetermined,

and efforts to prove a stable basis
for the solar system fail.

Quasi-Stellar Object

A candidate for a quasar has been detected
by the Infrared Astronomical Satellite:

IRAS 14348-1447 is the brightest, most
distant object in the Bright Galaxy Survey.

The strength of its emission is consistent
with a pattern of violent collisions

(molecular clouds in gas-rich spiral galaxies
that lead to rapid star formation)

and establishment of a dust-enshrouded object
whose raiment ultimately will be blown away

by stellar winds, by supernovae explosions,
by pressure from within the object itself.

For now, the shroud conceals much of the energy
generated by its spectacular, ultraluminous source.

The Very Large Telescope

will mark the completion, at last,
of nearly ten years' design. Soon to rise
on a peak in the Chilean desert,

the machine will consist of four
telescopes spaced along a hundred meters,
each telescope with an 8-meter wide

membrane of mirrored glass.
Supports will push and pull the membrane
to balance gravitational effects.

Inflatable, fabric domes will fold
down to open the instruments to the night
sky, enabling them to point

as one into the collecting area.
To focus all four on the same subject,
to combine their light in phase,

will be ambitious in the extreme.
If it works, astronomers might achieve
resolutions sufficient to study

galactic nuclei—to see,
in fine detail, the turmoil of matter
at the birth of stars.

The Brilliant Death of a Giant Star

has opened a window in space,
letting man view, for the first
time, the creation of matter.

The supernova, which exploded
within the large Magellanic Cloud,
is yielding secrets of celestial

lives and of fundamental elements.
This first close supernova to
appear in 400 years began

as the 10 million-year-old star
Sanduleak 69.202, once 20 times
the size of the sun. The stellar

body blew apart over 160,000
years ago, when it exhausted its
fuel of light and collapsed into

itself. Initial debris from the
progenitor star is dissipating.
Signs of the event, so far away,

did not reach Earth till 1987,
and scientists were surprised that
this big blue star should become

a supernova. In the last million
years of its life, Sanduleak expanded
from a big blue object into a red

supergiant, then lost some of its
matter and reverted to the smaller
blue state, with a heavy core.

Though its light is fading,
in a year we should be able to see
the dense, central remnant,

an infant neutron star.

Vast Problem Still Obscure

Most of the mass of the universe
may be contained in dark matter.
No one knows what that may be.

Astronomers say we could be
dealing with planetary objects
unable to produce luminosity;

some believe we are looking
at black holes or other things
formed when stars are born or die.

(For physicists, the heart
of dark matter lies in axions,
strings, magnetic monopoles.)

If related to stars, dark matter
presumably will be found where
stars are. If indeed exotic,

it won't react with matter
as we know it nor, likely,
with itself; and surely

it will, in any case,
have nothing at all to do
with everyday matter.

Lou Frank Proposed 2 Years Ago

that tiny comets may be pummeling us
20 times a minute, comets then visible only
to Frank and his ultraviolet camera

on the Dynamics Explorer. Now a second
satellite has recorded their effect on Earth's
outer regions. A telescope has glimpsed

the odd little bodies swarming between
Earth and the moon's orbit. According to Dr.
Frank, the elusive objects are made of

pure water-ice, dense as uncompacted
snow—90% emptiness. They fall apart and
disappear unnoticed at the merest tug

from a tidal force. The comets are
cloaked in a thin, black substance that is
nearly impervious to detection and

prevents their melting in space
from the sun's heat. Mini-comets coming
steadily since the start of the solar

system could account for the oceans.

The National Atmospheric Administration's

Space Laboratory warns that magnetic storms
caused by large solar flares could arrive any time.

The huge sun-spot related explosions hurl X-rays,
charged particles and hot gases toward Earth,

altering the shape of the ionosphere. Arriving
protons will touch spacecraft, increase drag,

affect orbits, weaken power systems, cause
lights to flicker, and interfere with contact

between airliners and ground control. The flares,
they say, pose no direct threat to life.

Theorists May No Longer Believe

in the balance of nature, the assumption that
normality inheres in equilibrium, an idea

that once governed the management of Earth's
resources and led to the idea that nature

knows best. On many levels, external forces
appear seldom to let things remain as they

are. Climate, for instance, has varied wildly
for two million years, eon to eon, decade

to decade, and at all scales between. Change
is the rule, the continuum being one of

disturbance, turmoil, fluctuation. There may
exist over millenia only a kind of floating

stasis of recurrent similarities. Perhaps one
cannot even imagine a time in balance.

III

In the 97th Execution Since the Restoration

of the death penalty, Leslie Lowenfield, a welder
from Guyana, was electrocuted today. Mr. Lowenfield

had barged into his ex-girlfriend's house in the out-
skirts of New Orleans and shot the occupants

as they ate boiled crabs at the kitchen table.
Lowenfield's lawyer argued that her client was a victim

of schizophrenia and could not understand the concept
of execution nor why he should be executed.

But Mr. Lowenfield refused to let her enter
a plea of insanity. He believed he was in Jacksonville,

Fla., at the time of the slaughter. In his final hours,
Lowenfield was visited by various friends,

by spiritual advisors and by Dale Brown,
Louisiana State's chief basketball coach, who had

been corresponding with Lowenfield since touring
death row with the LSU team 4 years ago.

Over the Weekend, Rich Masters and His Wife,

of Lakewood, Colo., mowed their lawn and
wrote a note for the mailman, instructing him

to contact the sheriff's office through
a portable phone placed in their mail-box,

with fifty dollars for his trouble,
the message explaining as well how to enter

the house, where to find the two
of them and names of family members to call,

—all wills, driver's licenses and other
important papers having been put in easy

reach. It seems the middle-aged couple had
spread a quilt, a blanket and shower curtain over

a love-seat, so it would not be stained,
and, facing one another, each holding a gun,

pulled the triggers. According to Captain
Blackhurst of Jefferson County, neighbors

said the pair had been married
for many years and were very close.

Lawrence Singleton Lives in a Trailer,

tending his yard in a remote corner of the San
Quentin compound. He keeps a nighttime curfew,

visits a psychologist weekly. "We hardly know
he's out there", says Parole Officer David

Langerman. "When he needs to shop, he lets us
know. Technically, we escort him, but anyone on

the streets has more to fear from the unknown
than from this little burned-out guy."

In three weeks, Mr. Singleton will be given
early release for good behavior and will be under

no obligation to tell officials his whereabouts
nor to take any longer the medication that

would sicken him if he drank alcohol.
According to Langerman, Singleton is wholly

defused and says he doesn't even need the drug—
he doesn't lose that much control. "I never

live in the past", says Mr. Singleton. After ten
years in prison, the once burly 60-year-old

still maintains he was mistaken for someone else.
Miss Mary Vincent says she still fears

the man who raped her and cut off her arms.

New Year's at 8:30 P.M. on Queen's Blvd.

the blue sedan of Carlyle Thompson hit three people
who, crossing from north to south, had stepped

off the median into a passing lane. The dead were
identified as Russian émigrés Aron Mirzayeva,

a leather worker; his wife, Mira, an accountant;
and a daughter, Alla, 16. According to friends

who gathered later to grieve, the family, recently
from Tashkent, had just earned enough money

to move into a 2-bedroom rental on Hoover Ave.
and place all four daughters in schools. Alla,

the youngest, and her sister Alexandra had found
weekend jobs at a neighborhood doughnut shop.

Mrs. Mirzayeva's 80-yr.-old mother recalled that,
on Friday night, her daughter and son-in-law had

gone to pick up Alexandra, who was doing an extra,
3-to-9 shift for a friend. Perhaps for company,

they took Alla with them. A bustling thoroughfare
that bisects the borough, Queens Boulevard is one of

the deadliest streets in the city, tied for fatalities
with the Bronx's Grand Concourse and Brooklyn's

Eastern Parkway. The broad, smooth esplanade-
design lures drivers into thinking they're on a free-

way. At times 200 feet wide, the Blvd.'s six lanes are difficult to cross on foot in the single stretch

of a traffic light. Yet people try and, in a rush, will run it in the dark, at mid-block.

Evidence Collected by Soubrenie *Et Al.*
in Their Ed.

of the essays of Hermine v. Hug-Hellmuth throws new light
on her murder by an orphaned nephew who felt betrayed

and manipulated by the analyst and could not forgive her
using him as a subject in writing "Aus dem Seelenleben

des Kindes", "A Study of the Mind of the Child", 1913.
In 1924, at eighteen, he strangled her. Arrested carrying

money and a watch, Rolf confessed. Analyst I. Sadger, once
the boy's tutor, testified that little could be done with human

beings after childhood. The judge called psychoanalysis
a fiction and ordered 12 years' solitary confinement with

days of darkness on the crime's anniversaries. The youth
obtained early release and sought support from the Vienna

Psychoanalytic Society on grounds of being a victim of
the talking cure. Told to sort out his problems with analyst

Helene Deutsch, who had not been consulted, Rolf began to
stalk her—and she engaged a bodyguard. Though those in

Freud's circle knew Hug-Helmuth as the messenger of his
theory that human personality fully forms before the age of

five, there was little reaction to her death in that quarter.
R. v. Urbantschitsch wrote in the women's pages of Neue

Freie Presse: "Now she is dead. Precisely the nephew whose
passions were featured in her books has relegated her

to silence". There was no mention of Hug-Hellmuth's "Tagebuch eines halbwüchsigen Mädchens", which, though fraudulent, had drawn praise from Freud, Stefan Zweig and Lou Andréas-Salomé for its evocation, in 1919, of the awakening senses of a female.

IV

The Love-Suicides at Sonezaki

was first performed in 1703, shortly after
the deaths that stirred Chikamatsu Monzaemon

to write his drama. Sometimes criticized
for its simple plot, the story of Ohatsu, a young

courtesan of the Temmaya Tea House, and Tokubei,
a poor clerk promised to someone else, is distinguished

by the beauty of the *michiyuki*, or love-journey,
of its final scene. In a brief, rarely included prologue,

Ohatsu visits the temples of Osaka looking for
solace. The text here consists of puns on sacred names,

prayers mixed with lyrics from the pleasure
quarter, fragments of classical poetry, and folk songs.

The music we shall hear is new, for the original
accompaniment of Ohatsu's mournful pilgrimage has

long been lost. The play also hints at the changing
theatre of the day: Ohatsu is represented by a delicate,

archaic one-man puppet of earlier times, while
other characters will be seen as complex and articulated

three-man Bunraku-type figures which suggest
the profound, conflicted emotions that moved the poet

and his contemporaries. Because they vividly
conveyed real events, the plays of Chikamatsu

were called 'living newspapers'.

Anak Agung Ayr Putu Rai, First-Born

of a royal caste, had a good life and was honored
when the streets of Denpasar were cleared

for strolling neighbors, guests and priests,
the chants of mourners, the beat of the gamelan,

and the whirr of cameras wielded by tourists
wearing lizard-printed shorts. Visitors

clambered over cars and trucks. Vendors of
batik and palm-leaf hats sold film at high prices.

A likeness of Mrs. Rai presided over the procession.
To confuse her spirit and keep it from going

back home, the bearers, at intervals,
twirled her modest, one-tiered crematory tower

that once might have had a lavish, 9-stepped roof
representing all of heaven and the cosmos.

Atop a small hill, the lady's body was passed
to its noble sarcophagus—a wooden bull at the end

of a path of white serpentine cloth held by her
female relatives. A holy man prayed.

Gasoline-soaked banana-tree logs were
hammered into the bull's legs. The animal burst

into flame, and steam issued from its nostrils.
"Beautiful", said a woman from France.

The bull blazed, the Balinese chatted,
Mrs. Rai was released from her cage of flesh,

and the foreigners, followed by the hawkers,
returned to their buses. Cupped in

coconuts, Mrs. Rai's ashes were slipped
into silver bowls, her bones laid with offerings.

The tower, too, was consumed,
and its light cinders tossed to the sea.

Egyptologists Found Khufu's Royal Boat

carefully buried just south of the Great Pyramid.
Light, slim, 140 ft. long, with delicate, curved ends,

the craft was probably meant to carry Pharaoh's
spirit on an eternal day-voyage through the heavens.

The elegant vessel now floats in a special glass
museum above its former tomb and overlooks a

puzzling companion site where scientists have
bored a tiny hole through a giant limestone slab,

inserted a space-age probe and glimpsed another
ship, dismantled five millenia ago. Reed-strewn piles

of wood and pieces of fallen mortar were detected,
with ancient workmen's rough notations scratched on

darkened walls. Air drawn from the pit did not
smell of the expected Lebanon cedar nor of oils from

sacred plants. A beetle scurried over the mass
of timbers. Days later, Cairo reported the death of

Kamal el-Mallakh, who discovered the first
boat and had predicted a second would be found.

Life-Size Statues Smashed 2,000 Years Ago

are on display in Florence. Painstaking computer
techniques were used for costly restorations

now in dispute over attributions and worth
of the two female figures—one intact,

the other lacking a head—and two mounted
equestrians with many sections missing.

Historians identified the images as members
of Emperor Caligula's family, whose effigies,

including here the once glorious Livia Drusilla,
were defaced and buried, in keeping with

the Roman practice of *Damnatio Memoriae*.
The works were almost left interred

in fields near Pergola, where part of a gilded
horse was found and quickly re-buried.

The farmer said, "We were afraid for our father,
who, in order to see what it was,

touched the hoof".

As Wife, Empress and Then the Woman

Napoleon abandoned in quest of a son,
Josephine remained at Malmaison,
the fairy-tale château she fell heir to

soon after her wedding. As royalty,
she restored the legendary residence.
Left by Bonaparte, she transformed

its plain grounds into sweeping vistas
and bred the finest roses of her time.
Sponsor of major botanical expeditions,

she attempted to sample every extant
rose, eventually possessing Parson's Pink,
Slater's Crimson, Hume's Blush Tea-

Scented China, exotics that, through her
careful nurturance, bore the forebears
of today's ever-blooming cultivars.

Her gardeners selected for viability
and perfected the grafter's art, using
sturdy, wild-type *R. canina* as stock

for fragile scions. Josephine's passion
turned the whole of France into a cradle
of rose-growing. Redouté painted her

specimens. Taxonomists described
them. Yet the woman did not live to see
their publication. Malmaison passed

into other hands, and the nurseries all
vanished. Lacking the plans of their
conception, a recent attempt to recreate

them aborted. The House of Misfortune
is now a museum. Leaving it, one passes
the small public park, in a nearby

village, where—with a daughter—
Josephine is buried. A bed of
begonias surrounds her likeness.

No Figure Is More Venerated Than the Virgin

of Guadalupe, no person is more despised—this Easter
week—than Rolando de la Rosa, who has tinkered with the

image of the Patroness of Mexico. For a show at El Museo
del Arte Moderno here, the artist superimposed the face

and bare breasts of Marilyn Monroe on those of La
Guadalupana. Protests have forced removal of the work.

Talk of lynching de la Rosa has caused El Museo's director
to resign. G. Bustamante, President of the National

Association of Parents, said, "Our essence has been
profaned". The Virgin is the namesake of many children,

service stations, taco stands, and a brand of cooking
oil. Regularly invoked in street speech,

La Guadalupana hangs on every repair shop wall,
with soccer teams and naked ladies.

V

Blindsight May Best Describe the Vision

of *Spalax ehrenberghi*, a mole rat whose eye is
morphologically the most regressed of mammals'.

Great reduction in its imaging apparatus,
and lack of response to ordinary light, suggest

that *Spalax* is sightless, but studies of the small,
subcutaneous visual organ, concealed beneath

specialized hairs, show it to be sensitive
and well integrated with the brain. The mole rat's

daily tunnellings, barely subsurface, may
provide retinal exposure adequate to maintain

circadian rhythms, which are broken if the eyes
are removed. *Spalax* likely abandoned the acute

metabolic burden of a large eye and directed its
remnants toward enhancing a way of life that

met more basic demands. How these changes came
about is not known. They seem adaptations

to severe constraints imposed by need for food,
warmth and occasional procreation, in a solitary

species isolated in tenebrous domains.

Because They Live on Blood Alone, Vampires

are the most specialized of the *Phyllostomidae*,
possessing a nasal thermoreceptor, anti-clotting

saliva, a tongue that transfers blood to the mouth,
and kidneys that quickly offload plasma after meals.

Early vampires, drawn to the heat of infestations,
fed on eggs of screwworms and muscid flies

that nested in the wounds of large animals. Bats
thus gained chance access to blood and underwent

a dietary change marked by adaptations for
inconspicuous feeding: canines that clipped, blade-

thin incisors, teeth that punctured neatly. Sanguinivory
in bats probably arrived coincident with the rise of

unique, Neotropical New World Miocene mammals
that later vanished. For vampires, the subsequent

appearance of domestic stock may have been crucial,
with humans likely intermediates in the transition.

A Diet of Glass

Until now, the only vertebrates known
to feed exclusively on sponges were two or three

teleost fishes. A new study hints that
the hawksbill, too, a marine turtle that lives

among tropical corals, may be a dedicated spongivore.
Intestines of Caribbean hawksbills show masses

of spicules, opal needles almost 5 millimeters
long, embedded in the epithelia.

No vertebrate diet of comparable silica
content has been described. Though well defended,

this food source may yield to predation
by large, mobile turtles. Removal of huge

amounts of slow-growing sponges could, in turn,
accelerate reef change. Hawksbills thus

are endangered by their preference for Porifera
and, of course, by the tortoiseshell trade.

In Amber

The specimen, from the Cordillera Septentrional,
exhibits visual characteristics of natural

Dominican ambers. Tests verify authenticity,
as do color and hardness correlating

with the great age of La Toca materials.
The clear, yellow amber containing the one-inch frog

weighs an ounce. The frog's right arm is broken
at the far end of the humerus, the left leg at the tip

of the tibiofibula. Entombment of the frog
was probably traumatic. A predator may have brought it

to a nest in a resinous tree, where frog
and nest adhered to the resin, with decomposing bones

of other frogs, maggots, a large centipede.
The frog's skin and eyes remain intact, transparent.

Radiographs showing fine details of vomer, dentition,
vertebral column, pectoral and pelvic girdles

assign it to *Eleutherodactylus*. Among amber finds,
the frog is the third complete vertebrate,

the first amphibian, to be described. It documents
a diverse fauna on the island of Hispaniola

20 million years earlier than heretofore
believed. The frog is very fragile,

very quiet, very safe.

Henry Rothman Tried to Put into Words

why his plant had won the Rodney W. Jones
Memorial Award for Best Brassocattleya or

Brassolaeliocattleya. A retired direct-mail
advertiser from Larchmont, Mr. Rothman

asked, "Wouldn't you agree, there's majesty
in the way it holds itself?" The hybrid, once

a "two-inch pup" gotten from an Illinois
supplier, was among 5,000 in the Orchid

Show at The New York Botanical Garden,
where judges with rulers, magnifiers and

score sheets gathered for the whole day in
a hot basement. "Lou, come look! That's

barn-burning Fuchsia, if ever I saw it",
shouted an expert, over a Paphiopedalum.

"Mulch this", murmured someone else,
dismissing a skinny specimen. Visiting

the conservatory that bears her name, Enid
Haupt found the display beautiful. "That's

the great thing about flowers—you always
hope the next season will be even prettier."

Hundreds of certificates, trophies, ribbons
were given out, and the judges announced 3

First Class awards, which included Greater
New York Orchid Society's Vice President's

Award for the Best Plant Grown
on a Windowsill or Under Lights.

Not Everyone Fancies the Little

pollard, with its severed crown,
that caps in winter a shorn trunk
and bears in summer a clump of shoots.
For centuries, pollarding enabled,

in Europe, the taking of firewood
while sparing the tree. Today,
the practice helps restrain unruly
specimens that else might grow

too great. (A forced containment
sometimes pleases in itself.)
Quick-growing deciduous species
tolerant of extreme reduction

do well. The stripling is lopped
at 2 meters, then denuded above
and below. New shoots atop the trunk
must be regularly struck

away. The bolled individual is not
allowed to achieve height nor to
possess long, luxuriant limbs.
With vigilance, a club-like shape is

fostered and formal limits fixed.
Pruned in autumn, the pollard bares
in wintertime its plain, flat top. If cut
too early, rebel growths of showy

stems produce a head of giant
leaves that open bright, Medusa-
like, against the cold.

Greenland Was Once Transformed

by Norse who settled amid fierce gales
on a strip of land between ice and sea.
Fervent 10th c. Christians, they introduced
dairying, built stone chapels, and once

traded a live polar bear for a mainland bishop,
then vanished. Data on diet and livestock,
cut-marks on bones, ice core readings and
clues from sagas, now point to a climatic

shift, in which the settlers butchered
their only cows and their cherished hounds.
Scientists note that Norwegian house-
flies found in domestic sediments

were succeeded, when hearth-fires died,
by carrion insects, then outdoor flies.
Wraith-like females exhumed from church-
yards were dressed in the thin, low cut,

narrow-style gowns of their homeland.
Neighboring Thule indigenes meanwhile had
flourished on local game and easily taken
fish, their women buried lavishly in furs.